# GRE**PIRATES**RIO

## ALEX STEWART

**W**
**FRANKLIN WATTS**
LONDON·SYDNEY

First published in paperback in 2014

First published in 2013 by Franklin Watts

Copyright © Arcturus Holdings Limited

Franklin Watts
338 Euston Road
London
NW1 3BH

Franklin Watts Australia
Level 17/207 Kent Street, Sydney, NSW 2000

Produced by Arcturus Publishing Limited,
26/27 Bickels Yard, 151–153 Bermondsey Street, London SE1 3HA

Edited and designed by: Discovery Books Ltd.

Series concept: Joe Harris
Managing editor for Discovery Books: Laura Durman
Editor: Clare Collinson
Picture researcher: Clare Collinson
Designer: Ian Winton

Picture credits:
Alamy: p. 10 (Moviestore collection Ltd), p. 17 (Adrian Buck), pp. 20, 21 (AF archive), p. 23 (RIA Novosti), p. 24 (E. Katie Holm),
p. 25 (Lebrecht Music and Arts Photo Library); Corbis: p. 6 (JP Laffont/Sygma), p. 27 (Joel W. Rogers); Getty Images: pp. 9, 22
(Candela Foto Art/Kreuziger), p. 19 (Syfy); iStockphoto.com: p. 11l (davidf), p. 15 (carrollphoto); Photoshot: p. 26 (Band Photo/
uppa.co.uk), p. 29 (Idols); Rex Features: p. 4 (Everett Collection), p. 12 (c. W. Disney/Everett); Shutterstock Images: title (Tom Antos),
p. 5 (Paul McKinnon), p. 7l (Bronskov), p. 7r (Myotis), p. 8 (Richard Welter), p. 11r (StacieStauffSmith Photos), p. 14l (pzAxe),
p. 14r (Horimono), p. 16 (RCPPHOTO), p. 18t (Mariano Heluani), p. 18b (Pres Panayotov), p. 28 (yuanann); Wikimedia Commons: p. 13.
Cover images: Getty Images: top (Candela Foto Art/Kreuziger); iStockphoto.com: bottom centre (davidf); Shutterstock Images:
background (Patryk Kosmider).

A CIP catalogue record for this book is available from the British Library.

Dewey Decimal Classification Number: 364.1'64'09

ISBN: 978 1 4451 3753 7

Franklin Watts is a division of Hachette Children's Books, an Hachette UK company.
www.hachette.co.uk

Printed in China

SL002667UK
Supplier 03, Date 0614, Print Run 3625

# CONTENTS

Pirates! The word sent terror through the heart of every sailor that ever put to sea. From ancient times, pirates attacked and **plundered** ships in all the world's oceans. They took whatever they found, from gold to slaves, and often killed those who got in their way.

## SEA THIEF

Pirates were tough and ruthless seafarers who chose a life of battles and adventure on the high seas in the hope of becoming rich.

# FIGHTING TALK

## Buccaneers, corsairs and privateers

The word 'pirate' refers to all sea robbers, but there were several different types of pirate. Buccaneers were pirates operating in the Caribbean Sea in the 17th century. Corsairs attacked shipping in the southern Mediterranean, often from bases on the Barbary Coast in North Africa. Privateers had permission from their government to seize ships and **cargo** from enemy nations. Privateers were seen as heroes at home, but their victims saw them as pirates.

# TREASURE HUNTERS

Ever since **traders** sailed the seas, pirates preyed on their **vessels**. Over 2,500 years ago, pirates used fast warships called **biremes** to steal precious cargo from ancient Greek **merchant ships**. In Roman times, pirates stole valuable olive oil and grain, and took captives to sell as slaves. In the 16th century, ships bringing treasure from the Americas to Europe gave pirates rich and tempting new targets.

## PIRATE SHIP

From the 16th century, pirates often converted merchant ships, similar to this replica of the 18th-century HMS *Bounty*, into warships by equipping them with extra cannon.

# PIRATES OF THE GOLDEN AGE

In the 16th century, Spain conquered a vast empire in South and Central America. Soon, Spanish galleons began to bring vast quantities of gold and silver back to Europe. The vessels, laden with treasure, were easy targets for pirates, and the 'Golden Age of Piracy' began!

## FORTUNE HUNTERS

Life on board a trading ship was often harsh, and conditions and pay were poor. During the Golden Age of Piracy, many merchant seamen chose a life of adventure and piracy on the high seas instead.

## BAREFOOT PIRATE

In warm climates, pirates and sailors often went barefoot on board ship. This made it easier to climb the **rigging** to adjust the sails.

## TELESCOPE

The telescope was a vital piece of equipment when it came to deciding whether or not a nearby ship was worth attacking.

# SPANISH TREASURE

In 1545 and 1546, Spanish conquerors found gold and silver mines in South America and Mexico. On its way back to Spain, the precious metal had to pass by the Caribbean islands of Jamaica, Barbados and Hispaniola. Here, nests of pirates lay in wait.

## PIECES OF EIGHT

During the 1590s, Spain shipped nearly 3 million kg (7 million lb) of silver and gold out of South America. Much of this **loot** was in the form of coins, such as silver dollars and gold **doubloons**. Silver dollars were known as '**pieces of eight**', because each was worth one eighth of a Spanish dollar.

## PRECIOUS CHEST

Sometimes pirates got lucky and captured a ship transporting chests of gold and silver coins.

# BATTLE REPORT

### HMS *Scarborough* vs John Martel

Captain John Martel was one of the most ruthless pirates in the Caribbean in the early 18th century. He plundered vessels off the coast of Jamaica and is said to have killed all the sailors aboard one of the ships he preyed on. In 1717, a 30-gun British warship, the HMS *Scarborough*, finally trapped Martel and his ship near the island of Santa Cruz. Martel set fire to his ship rather than let it be captured. He then managed to escape and was never seen again.

# BLOODY BUCCANEERS

In the 17th century, most of the buccaneers preying on Spanish ships in the Caribbean were British, French or Dutch. Hoping to become rich from stolen treasure, they set up pirate bases on the islands of Tortuga and Jamaica.

## PIRATES' PRIZE

From their coastal strongholds, buccaneers had clear views of the open sea and the vessels upon it. When a treasure ship came near, they sailed out to capture their prize.

# PIRATES OF PORT ROYAL

Of all the pirate bases in the Caribbean, Port Royal was the most famous. The English captured the island of Jamaica from the Spanish in 1655. To defend it, the English government invited buccaneers, known as the 'Brethren of the Coast', to settle in its capital, Port Royal. By the 1680s, over 6,000 people lived there and some 200 ships visited each year. The town swarmed with **bandits** and its pubs did a roaring trade as pirates spent their **ill-gotten** loot.

## BROTHERHOOD OF BUCCANEERS

Buccaneers in Port Royal formed a group called the 'Brethren of the Coast'.

## FIGHTING TALK

### Henry Morgan – the swashbuckling knight

Sir Henry Morgan was the most famous of all buccaneers in Port Royal. He served in the British Royal Navy before becoming a successful privateer, preying on Spanish ships during England's war with Spain. In 1671, with over 1,000 men, he attacked the Spanish city of Panama in Central America. He captured over 400,000 pieces of eight and the city was destroyed by fire. England had made peace with Spain in 1670, so Morgan was arrested for his illegal raid. However, instead of punishment, he was given a knighthood by King Charles II!

# TRICKS AND TERROR

With pirates, there was no such thing as a fair fight. They used every possible trick to seize a ship and win their prize. The most important **tactic** in a pirate attack was surprise. The second was to scare the victim into handing over the loot.

## SURPRISE!

Pirates planned their attacks carefully so they could take their victims by surprise. Sometimes they flew the same flag as their prey, pretending to be from the same nation. They often disguised their ships as innocent merchant vessels by **camouflaging** their **gun ports**. In this way, they could approach their target before throwing off their disguise and attacking.

## PIRATES IN HIDING

Pirates often lurked in narrow inlets along rocky shores before attacking an unsuspecting vessel.

# TERROR AND THREATS

When it was too late for a target vessel to get away, pirates would hoist the pirate flag – known as the Jolly Roger. Many sailors would surrender as soon as they saw the terrifying flag. Once aboard their prey, pirates often threatened violence to make their victims hand over anything of value.

## THE JOLLY ROGER

Pirates often flew plain black flags, but the Jolly Roger was sometimes black and white, and marked with a frightening image such as a skull and crossed bones or swords.

## YOUR JEWELS OR YOUR FINGERS!

To get their captives' rings, some pirates threatened to cut off victims' fingers!

# FIGHTING TALK

## The gentleman pirate

Pirates' tactics were not always successful. Stede Bonnet, also known as 'the gentleman pirate' because of his family's wealth, was caught by his own tactic of hiding his ship up rivers. In 1718, Colonel William Rhett cornered Bonnet in the Cape Fear River, captured him and handed him over to the law for **execution**.

# BLACKBEARD

**No pirate was more feared than Edward Teach, also known as Blackbeard. From 1716 until his death in 1718, this notorious pirate terrorized merchant seamen in the Caribbean and along the east coast of America.**

## BLACKBEARD'S FLEET

Blackbeard was an English privateer who joined a group of Caribbean pirates in 1716. By 1718, he commanded his own 40-gun warship, the *Queen Anne's Revenge*, and eight other ships. With nine ships in his fleet, he had his own small navy!

### TERROR OF THE SEAS

For two long years, Blackbeard, played here by Ian McShane in the film *Pirates of the Caribbean: On Stranger Tides*, struck terror in the hearts of innocent sailors. Most of his victims surrendered at the sight of his flag!

# FEARSOME APPEARANCE

Blackbeard worked hard to create a terrifying image. He had a long, thick, black beard, which he is said to have twisted into pigtails and tied with coloured ribbons. According to some accounts, before battle he tucked slow-burning fuses under his hat, so smoke would swirl up around his face.

## BLACKBEARD VS LIEUTENANT MAYNARD

In this painting by Jean Leon Jerome Ferris (1920), Blackbeard is seen fighting in his last-ever battle, with Lieutenant Robert Maynard. Blackbeard was killed and his head was hung up for all to see.

# BATTLE REPORT

### Battle of Ocracoke Bay, 1718

In 1718, Blackbeard was cornered off the coast of North Carolina, North America, by Lieutenant Robert Maynard of the Royal Navy. A fierce hand-to-hand battle was fought. Wielding his **cutlass**, Blackbeard broke Maynard's sword, but was slashed across the neck by one of Maynard's men. Blackbeard fought on until, wounded 25 times, he eventually fell down dead. His reign of terror was over.

# ARMED TO THE TEETH

To capture a ship, pirates needed to have deadly hand-held weapons, so they armed themselves with the best they could steal. These included daggers, knives, swords and cutlasses, as well as **pistols** and **muskets**.

## ARMED FOR ATTACK

Pirates often carried a variety of weapons into battle. They used them to defend themselves as well as to fight for their prize.

## FLINTLOCK PISTOL

**Flintlock** pistols were among the most valued of all pirate weapons. Their small size and light weight meant they could easily be carried when boarding a ship.

# FIGHTING TALK

## Flintlocks

Pirate pistols and muskets were flintlocks. Pulling the **trigger** hit a splinter of flint against a piece of steel. This caused a shower of sparks that lit gunpowder in a 'pan' – creating a 'flash in the pan'. This set off the main charge that drove the bullet out of the barrel. Re-loading was time-consuming, so pirates often carried several pistols and other weapons. It is said that Blackbeard carried six pistols tied to his belt.

# SWORD SHAPES

Many pirates were very skilled swordsmen. They used various types of swords. The **rapier** had a long, thin blade with a lethally sharp point. It was designed for stabbing. The cutlass had a heavier, curved blade, designed for cutting and slashing.

## SWORD FIGHT
This pirate has a rapier in his right hand and an ordinary sword in the left. If his slender rapier breaks, he can continue with the shorter, heavier weapon.

# SHIP AHOY!

From ancient biremes powered by oars, to well-armed warships driven by the wind, pirate vessels needed to be fast and sturdy. In the Golden Age of Piracy, many pirate ships were captive merchant vessels converted for war.

## PRIZED WARSHIP

From the 16th century, **frigates** were among the most prized of all pirate ships. These warships were built for speed and could carry up to 40 cannon and 250 crew.

## MAST

Frigates had three masts, each with several sails attached.

## SAILS

The sails on some large frigates weighed as much as 10,000 kg (22,000 lb) and had a total area of 8,000 sq m (10,000 sq yd).

## YARD

Yards were wooden poles from which the sails were suspended. They were fixed horizontally to the masts.

## RIGGING

The ropes that formed the ship's rigging were used to support the masts and control the sails.

# TRADING UP

Pirate captains often started off in small ships, but traded up to larger and more powerful vessels as they became more successful. They often converted the ships they seized to make them more suitable for piracy, for example by removing cabins to make more room for cannon.

## STEADY AS SHE GOES!

On board a pirate ship, the helmsman, or pilot, was in charge of the steering. He worked closely with the **navigator** and lookout. Dozens of men, over 100 on large vessels, were also needed for tasks such as raising and lowering the sails and anchor.

## COMBAT STATS

*Queen Anne's Revenge* - Blackbeard's flagship
- **Type of vessel:** frigate
- **Original name:** *Concord*
- **Length:** about 27 m (90 ft)
- **Width:** about 8 m (25 ft)
- **Weight:** 3300,000 kg (660,000 lb)
- **No of masts:** 3
- **Crew:** up to 250 pirates on board
- **Guns:** 40 cannon

# TAKE AIM ... FIRE!

The cannon was the pirate's deadliest weapon. The largest cannon, known as demi-cannon, weighed 1,500 kg (3,400 lb) and could fire a lead ball right through the side of a ship. The smallest, known as 2-pounders, weighed 270 kg (600 lb) and could kill two men with one 2-pound (1-kg) shot.

## WHEELED CARRIAGE

Big cannon like this weighed as much as 1,500 kg (3,300 lb)! They were put on wheeled carriages, so they could be rolled forwards for firing in battle.

## CONVERTED FOR BATTLE

When pirates captured a merchant vessel, they would often convert it for their own use by cutting rows of gun ports in the hull and equipping it with cannon. This meant they were more heavily armed than most of their opponents.

## GUN PORT

As well as those on the upper decks, cannon were also kept on lower decks. These helped prevent the ship from capsizing. The guns were positioned behind gun ports, which were opened for battle.

# CANNON FODDER

As well as round lead balls that could smash through a ship's **hull**, cannon could be loaded with all kinds of **missiles**. Two cannon balls joined together with a chain were good for smashing rigging. Grape shot (small iron balls packed in bags) was effective against people at close range. Canister shot (lead or iron balls, gravel and nails in a metal container) was even more deadly. Sangrenel (cloth bags full of jagged pieces of metal) produced a cloud of flying metal that could inflict horrible wounds.

## CANNON CREW

It took at least three men to load and fire most cannon.

## COMBAT STATS

**The 32-pounder**
- Diameter of barrel: 130 mm (5 in)
- Weight of shot: 14.5 kg (32 lb)
- Weight of gunpowder needed to fire: 8 kg (18 lb)
- Range: 1,000 m (1,200 yd)
- Number of men 1 shot could kill: at least 10

**The 6-pounder**
- Diameter of barrel: 76 mm (3 in)
- Weight of shot: 2.7 kg (6 lb)
- Weight of gunpowder needed to fire: 2.7 kg (6 lb)
- Range: 1,645 m (1,800 yd)
- Number of men 1 shot could kill: 3

# ATTACK!

If a merchant vessel chose not to surrender when a pirate ship approached, the attack began. First came the cannon fire. Then the pirates came alongside and boarded. This is when these great warriors were at their most terrifying.

## CANNON FIRE

Pirates did not generally want to sink the ships they attacked, as they hoped to steal them or their cargo. Warning shots were usually fired at first. If the victims did not surrender, the attackers then fired their cannon at the masts and rigging. Sometimes, they attacked with a 'broadside' – firing all the guns on one side of their ship at the same time.

# COMING ABOARD!

With the target ship disabled, the pirates sailed alongside and, armed with deadly weapons, they boarded. Some crossed on planks, some jumped, others swung into battle on ropes. Fierce hand-to-hand fighting often followed. Brave merchant seamen battled for their lives as well as their ship and its cargo, but pirates were unlikely to spare anyone who dared to resist them.

# BATTLE REPORT

## Fatal attack

In May 1722, the Italian pirate Matthew Luke attacked the English warship HMS *Launceston* in the dark. He thought it was a merchant ship – fatal mistake! The pirates were captured, taken to Jamaica and hanged. Luke confessed to taking four British ships and murdering all of their crew. One of the pirates, a Spaniard, claimed to have slain 20 Englishmen with his own hands.

# STOLEN TREASURE

Pirates pillaged ships for anything of value. Hoards of gold, silver and jewels were the most prized of all booty. Almost as precious were colourful silks and spices, such as cloves, pepper and nutmeg, from the Far East.

## PRECIOUS CARGO

There are lots of stories of pirates keeping their treasure in chests, which they buried on remote islands. Treasure was often transported in chests, but in reality pirates rarely buried their loot. They usually couldn't wait to enjoy their ill-gotten gains.

# BURIED TREASURE

One pirate known to have buried his treasure was Captain William Kidd, a Scottish privateer. In 1698, Kidd captured the *Quedah Merchant* in the Indian Ocean, with its cargo of silk and other precious goods. On his journey back to North America, Kidd was accused of being a pirate. He hid some of his treasure by burying it on Gardiner's Island, and then claimed he was innocent. The booty was found and Kidd was hanged. Before his execution, Kidd said he buried another vast hoard somewhere in the 'Indies'. Treasure hunters have been looking for it ever since!

## LOOT FOR LOADING

Some pirates raided coastal towns, taking anything they found, including casks of food and drink. Here, in a scene from the film *Aybolit-66*, stolen goods are piled high on a beach, ready for loading onto the pirates' ship.

# FIGHTING TALK

## Piracy's greatest hoard

In 1694, the English pirate Henry Every and his crew attacked a treasure ship belonging to the Grand Moghul of India. They took precious metals and gems worth an estimated £600,000, or £250 million in today's money. The loot made Every the richest pirate in the world and has been called the greatest hoard in the history of piracy.

# PIRATE WOMEN

Throughout history, there have been women who sought adventure and fortune on the high seas. Women wielded swords and cutlasses alongside other pirates. Some even commanded their own pirate fleets.

## PIRATE COMMANDER

Grace O'Malley, shown here as she may have looked, was the proud Irish commander of three pirate ships. The daughter of a sea captain, she became an expert sailor at a young age and gained a reputation as a fierce fighter.

## FIGHTING TALK

### Pirate meets queen

In 1593, Grace O'Malley's son and half-brother were taken captive by the English. Grace, now aged 63, sailed to England to ask Queen Elizabeth I for their release. The queen agreed to meet her and was so impressed by this remarkable warrior that she granted all of Grace's requests and allowed her to continue her life of piracy!

# PIRATES IN DISGUISE

In 1720, a pirate ship captained by the notorious 'Calico Jack' Rackham was engaged in battle off the coast of Jamaica. Two of Rackham's crew were women dressed as men. With most of their shipmates below deck, Anne Bonny and Mary Read fought hard to defend the ship. The battle was fierce, but eventually the crew was captured and condemned to death.

## ANNE BONNY AND MARY READ

When Irish woman Anne Bonny (left) fell in love with the pirate 'Calico Jack' Rackham, she decided to join his crew. On board his ship, she found Mary Read. Disguised as a man, Read had served in the British Army before becoming a pirate.

# ESCAPE FROM EXECUTION

Anne and Mary were both pregnant when captured, so escaped execution. Anne managed to get away and some say she had 10 children and lived to the age of 80. Mary died in prison, possibly during childbirth.

# THE PIRATE KNIGHT

Sir Francis Drake was the first English sea captain to sail round the world and a pirate with royal approval! Before England's war with Spain (1585–1604), Drake stole Spanish treasure worth many millions in today's money.

## GOING ASHORE

Francis Drake first tried his hand at piracy in 1572–73. Having sailed to Central America, he and his crew went ashore. They ambushed a mule train in Panama that was transporting Spanish treasure. They captured over 20,000 kg (45,000 lb) of gold and silver, and made off with as much as they could carry.

### GENTLEMAN PIRATE
Francis Drake (played here by Patrick McAlinney) was a hero to the English, but a pirate to the Spanish.

# ROYALLY REWARDED

Between 1577 and 1580, Drake made the second ever round-the-world voyage. On his way, with permission from Queen Elizabeth I, he plundered Spanish ships and bases. On his return, Elizabeth took a large share of the loot and gave Drake a knighthood!

## THE *GOLDEN HINDE*
When it returned home in 1580, Drake's 22-gun ship was probably the richest ever to sail into a British port.

## MAIN MAST
Drake's galleon had three masts. The main mast in the centre was 28 m (92 ft) high.

## SAIL
Drake's ship had five square sails, with a total sail area of 386 sq m (4,150 sq ft).

## HULL
The *Golden Hinde* had a wooden hull 31 m (102 ft) long and 7 m (22 ft) wide. It had a sailing speed of 9 knots (15 km/h or 9 mph).

## COMBAT STATS

**Round-the-world loot**

- **From the first ship Drake attacked:** gold worth 25,000 Spanish dollars, worth about £7 million today
- **From the *Cacafuego* treasure ship:** 36 kg (80 lb) of gold, 26,000 kg (57,000 lb) of silver, 13 cases of coins, pearls, jewellery, precious stones
- **Drake's share:** from the whole voyage, £10,000 (more than £10 million today)
- **Crew's share:** from the whole voyage, £8,000 (more than £8 million today) shared between them
- **Queen's share:** enough to pay off all her debts and have £42,000 (over £42 million today) left over

# PIRATES OF THE CHINA SEAS

From the Mediterranean to the Atlantic, the Pacific and the Indian Ocean, pirates have plundered ships in all the world's seas. Some of the largest and most powerful pirate fleets operated in the waters of Southeast Asia.

## CHEN ZUYI

In the 14th century, Chen Zuyi was the most feared pirate in Southeast Asia. With 5,000 men under his command, he terrorized traders in the Straits of Malacca (linking the Pacific and Indian Oceans) for many years. He was finally captured in 1407 by a Chinese voyager named Zheng He.

### ZHENG HE – PIRATE DEFEATER

Zheng He was a mariner who utterly destroyed Chen Zuyi's pirate fleet. Chen was sent back to China for public execution.

# PIRATE QUEEN

The largest pirate fleet of all time was led by a Chinese pirate named Ching Shih. With her vast 'Red Flag Fleet', and many thousands of pirates under her control, she dominated the South China Sea in the early 19th century. She retired from piracy in 1810, when she accepted an **amnesty**. She negotiated **pardons** for most of her men, kept all her fortune and ran a gambling den until her death at the age of 69.

## UNDEFEATED COMMANDER

The character Mistress Ching, seen here in the film *Pirates Of The Caribbean: At World's End*, was based on Ching Shih, perhaps the greatest pirate of all. A brilliant and ruthless commander, she remained undefeated against the Chinese, British and Portuguese navies.

## COMBAT STATS

**Ching Shih's Red Flag Fleet**
- **Location:** South China Sea
- **Active:** 1805–1810
- **Size of fleet:** over 1,800 ships
- **Number of pirates:** 70,000–80,000 – over 17,000 directly under Ching Shih's command, the rest being made up of other pirate groups who worked with her fleet

29

# GLOSSARY

**Amnesty** An agreement by officials to take no action against someone who has committed an offence.

**Bandit** An outlaw or robber.

**Bireme** An ancient ship with two rows of oarsmen on each side.

**Camouflage** To disguise or cover up.

**Cargo** The goods carried on board a ship.

**Cutlass** A sword with a thick, curved blade.

**Doubloon** A Spanish gold coin.

**Execution** Being put to death.

**Flintlock** A gun fired by a spark from a flint.

**Frigate** A small, fast warship.

**Galleon** A large sailing ship with three or more masts, used especially by Spain in the 15th to 17th centuries.

**Gun port** An opening in the side of a ship from which guns could be fired.

**Hull** The body of a ship.

**Ill-gotten** Taken by illegal means.

**Loot** Stolen goods.

**Merchant ship** A type of ship used for transporting goods for trade.

**Missile** An object that is fired from a weapon.

**Musket** An early form of rifle.

**Navigator** The sailor who directs the route of a ship.

**Pardon** A release from punishment.

**Piece of eight** Silver coin worth one eighth of a Spanish dollar.

**Pistol** A gun that could be held and fired with one hand.

**Plunder** To steal goods by force.

**Rapier** A sword with a thin, pointed blade.

**Rigging** The ropes that support a ship's masts and sails.

**Tactic** The way a plan, such as a battle plan, is carried out.

**Trader** A person who buys and sells goods.

**Trigger** The piece of metal that operates the firing mechanism in a gun.

**Vessel** A ship.

# FURTHER INFORMATION

## Books

Brown, Martin and Deary, Terry. *Horrible Histories Handbook: Pirates*. Scholastic, 2006.

Chrisp, Peter. *Pirates* (Navigators). Kingfisher, 2011.

Lassieur, Allison. *The History of Pirates: From Privateers to Outlaw*. Capstone Press, 2006.

Malam, John. *You Wouldn't Want to Be a Pirate's Prisoner!* Franklin Watts, 2012.

Matthews, John. *Pirates: Rogues' Gallery*. Carlton, 2007.

Riley, Peter. *Pirates*. Scholastic, 2007.

Savery, Annabel. *Pirates* (It's Amazing). Franklin Watts, 2011.

Taplin, Sam and McNee, Ian. *Pirate's Handbook*. Usborne, 2009.

## Websites

*A General History of the Pyrates*
**http://digital.lib.ecu.edu/historyfiction/item.aspx?id=joh**
An online edition of an 18th-century book about pirates by Daniel Defoe, author of *Robinson Crusoe*.

Maritime Pirate History
**www.piratesinfo.com/**
A very comprehensive site with an interesting discussion forum.

Pirates
**www.rmg.co.uk/explore/sea-and-ships/facts/ships-and-seafarers/pirates**
From the Royal Museums at Greenwich, a brief, no-nonsense site of wise words and clear information.

The Pirate Ship
**www.the-pirate-ship.com/index.html**
A light-hearted and generally accurate site, packed with information for younger children.

# Index